SUSTAINING OUR ENVIRONMENT

Tourism

Rufus Bellamy

W
FRANKLIN WATTS
LONDON•SYDNEY

First published in 2009 by
Franklin Watts
338 Euston Road
London NW1 3BH

Franklin Watts Australia
Level 17/207 Kent Street
Sydney NSW 2000

Series editor: Adrian Cole
Art Director: Jonathan Hair
Design: Simon Borrough
Picture Research: Diana Morris

Acknowledgements:
Stuart Abraham/Alamy: 29. Suzanne Bickerdike/Shutterstock: 26. Blue Flag International
(blueflag.org): 20. Chris de Bode/Panos: 15. Jocelyn Carlin/Panos: 39. T Costin/istockphoto:
16b. Ozgur Denmaz/istockphoto: 14. Elena Elisseeva/istockphoto: 10. Empowering Women
of Nepal (3sistersadventure.com/ewn): 36. Christopher Ewing/istockphoto: 16t. Simon
Gurney/istockphoto: 27. Martin Harvey/Corbis: 32. Gavin Hellier/Alamy: 41bl.
Hemis/Alamy: front cover. Fred Hoogervorst/Panos: 9. Image Bank/Getty Images: 31.
KJA/istockphoto: 19. Nomad Safaris (nomadsafaris.co.nz): 38. Nikolai Okhitin/istockphoto:
18. Jim Parkin/istockphoto: 12. Joerg Reuther/Alamy: 23. Jaime Roset/istockphoto: 8. Joel
Saget/Getty Images: 13. Skyrail Rainforest Cableway (skyrail.com.au): 23. Paul Smith/Panos:
37. Paul Souders/Corbis: 40. Stone/Getty Images; 28. Surfers Against Sewage: 21. Britta
Kasholm-Tengve/istockphoto: 30. Sven Torfinn/Panos: 34, 35. TRAFFIC India (traffic.org):
24. UNWTO: 41br. Geoff Williamson/Alamy: 17. Ariadne Van Zandbergen/PD: 25.
Every attempt has been made to clear copyright. Should there be any inadvertent omission
please apply to the publisher for rectification.

A CIP catalogue record for this book is available from the British Library.

Dewey number: 338.4'791

ISBN: 978 0 7496 8824 0

Printed in China

Franklin Watts is a division of Hachette Children's Books, an Hachette UK company.
www.hachette.co.uk

Contents

Tourism – the world's biggest industry

Every year hundreds of millions of people travel as tourists. Tourism is the biggest industry in the world, both in terms of the number of people it employs and the amount of money it generates. Because it is such a big business and supports so many jobs, its impact on the environment and on people is of great importance. This book looks at the key environmental and social issues linked with tourism and highlights what is being done to try and make tourism more sustainable.

Tourism can be large scale, like this, or it can be on a smaller scale, just involving independent travel. ▼

What is tourism?

There are many types of tourism. For example people might be cultural tourists and visit a city to explore its museums and other cultural treasures, or they might be sports tourists and go to a mountain resort in the winter to ski. Some tourists, known as independent travellers, plan their own itinerary; others use tour companies to arrange their holidays for them.

The tourism industry exists to service the need of tourists – for example, hotels provide tourists with a place to stay, tour guides show them the sites and visitor attractions provide them with things to see and do on holiday.

'Twenty years ago sustainable tourism was just an idea. Now it is entering the travel and tourism mainstream as more companies embrace new innovations demonstrating environmentally-friendly operations, a commitment to safeguarding the cultural and natural heritage of our planet, and addressing poverty alleviation through enlightened business practices.'

Costas Christ, Chairman of Judges, 2008 Tourism for Tomorrow Awards

Defining sustainable tourism

One of the most recent developments in the field of sustainable tourism is the Partnership for Global Sustainable Tourism Criteria (GSTC Partnership). This is a coalition of over 30 organisations that are working together to 'foster increased understanding of sustainable tourism practices and the adoption of universal sustainable tourism principles.'

The Partnership was initiated by the Rainforest Alliance, the United Nations Environment Programme (UNEP), the United Nations Foundation, and the United Nations World Tourism Organisation (UNWTO). According to the organisers, the GSTC criteria will be the minimum standard that 'any tourism business should aspire to reach in order to protect and sustain the world's natural and cultural resources while ensuring tourism meets its potential as a tool for poverty alleviation.'

Sustainability is based on:

- effective sustainability planning,

- maximizing social and economic benefits for the local community,

- enhancing cultural heritage,

- reducing negative impacts to the environment.

If planned well, tourism can help wildlife, such as the rhino. If done badly it can help to destroy it. ▼

What is sustainable tourism?

As you will find out in the rest of this book, tourists and the tourism industry can have a wide range of environmental and social impacts – some good, some bad. Sustainable tourism is an approach that tries to reduce the negative impacts to a manageable level and to make sure that both the natural environment and the local culture of a tourist destination do not suffer any significant or long-term damage. Sustainable tourism also tries to maximise the positive benefits of tourism. One widely used definition of sustainable tourism is 'tourism that meets the needs of present tourists and host regions while protecting and enhancing opportunity for the future'.

The transport question

Tourists travel almost by definition. At the local and national level tourist travel adds to traffic congestion, noise and air pollution. Globally, tourism is linked to the rapid growth in air travel (and the pollution that it produces) that has taken place in recent years. Tourism travel also uses vast amounts of fuel and other resources, and helps drive the expansion of airports and the development of new roads and other transport infrastructure – all of which have an environmental impact or 'footprint'.

Rises predicted

Tourist travel is expected to grow significantly in the future – the World Tourism Organisation (WTO) predicts that by 2020, international tourist arrival numbers will rise to more than 1.5 billion each year. Air transport already makes up the bulk of this tourism transport and its importance is set to rise.

Debate.....
Should tourists fly?

One of the most contentious issues in tourism travel is the environmental impact of flying. It is now considered to be the fastest growing source of carbon dioxide – a greenhouse gas thought to be accelerating climate change.

To help combat this problem, some environmental groups are now asking people to fly less and to use other forms of transport that produce less pollution. However, many people argue that tourism air travel only produces a small percentage of the total amount of greenhouse gas produced by human activity (around 2 per cent according to UNWTO's Climate Change and Tourism Report) and that the benefits that it brings, especially to less developed countries, outweighs the impact it could have on the climate.

Tourists queue at an airport terminal. Tourist travel can have a negative environmental impact.
▼

'Those who say: "Do not travel far from home and avoid taking planes to save several tons of carbon emissions," should think twice ... because these trips are often to countries that will be the first victims of warming ... These communities, like Bali, would be doubly affected if we also deprive them of the economic contribution of tourism.'

Statement by Francesco Frangialli, Secretary-General of the World Tourism Organisation, on the occasion of the United Nations Conference on Climate Change, 2007

Debate.....

Should tourists go to Antarctica?

Antarctica is one of the last unspoiled wildernesses in the world, but even here tourism is beginning to have an impact. In 2007/8, over 40,000 tourists visited the region, many of them in large cruise ships.

Much of the tourism in Antarctica is, at present, self-regulated by the International Association of Antarctic Tour Operators (IAATO). This group has put in place a series of guidelines for both its members and for visitors to limit the impact of tourism on the fragile Antarctic environment.

Despite this, concerns have been raised about the possibility of accidents and the problems that could be caused by tourism groups that do not abide by IAATO guidelines.

Carbon offsetting

One option that is being put forward as a way of reducing the environmental impact of tourism air travel is 'carbon offsetting'. Many companies and organisations are providing tourists with services that they claim counterbalance (or offset) the carbon dioxide emitted by a tourist's journey. Such services include tree planting (growing trees lock up carbon dioxide) or the development of energy efficiency schemes in developing countries. While many of these schemes do help conservation, some have been criticised as being ineffective and poorly monitored.

This graph shows how worldwide tourism numbers are expected to grow (in millions). Tourist traffic can bring problems, including traffic congestion.

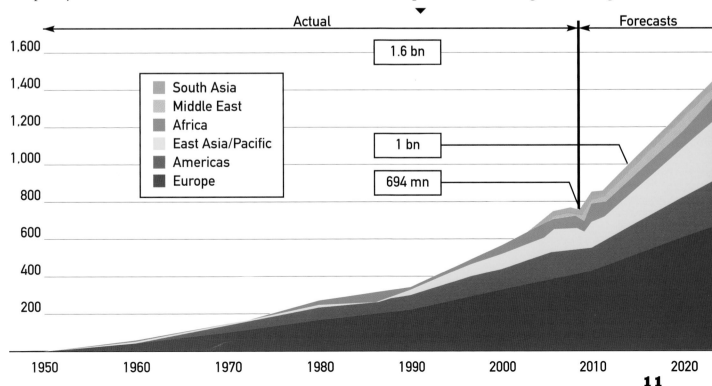

| | Actual | Forecasts |

1,600 — 1.6 bn

South Asia
Middle East
Africa
East Asia/Pacific
Americas
Europe

1 bn

694 mn

1,400
1,200
1,000
800
600
400
200

1950 1960 1970 1980 1990 2000 2010 2020

Travelling light

The environmental impact of tourist travel is based on two main things – how far people go and how they make their journeys. If a person uses a bicycle or a train to get to a holiday destination close to where they live, then they will have a much smaller environmental impact (or 'footprint') than someone who travels a long distance by car or by air.

Impact reduction

The transport issue does not end when a person gets to their destination. People on holiday can choose environmentally friendly ways of getting around (for example, on foot) or more damaging options (for example, hire cars or even helicopter tours).

Around the world, there are many projects trying to reduce the environmental impact of tourism travel. Often these are linked to general plans to try and make transport more sustainable. For example, China invested over a billion US dollars expanding its Beijing underground public transport system in the run-up to the 2008 Olympics. Today, this allows both tourists and residents to travel around the city without using cars or taxis long after the Olympics.

Other schemes aim to get tourists to use cleaner forms of transport. For example, in Paris many tourists are taking advantage of a new bike hire scheme called *la Vélorution*. This has a network of hundreds of bike hire stations across the city, which allows tourists and residents to travel cheaply and with zero emissions.

> **'If you … reduce your pace, even a little, you too will get to see, smell, taste, hear and feel the world.'**
>
> UNEP Green Passport, explaining the appeal of slow travel

▼ **The greenest form of tourism travel is on two wheels or two feet.**

Case study······ Let the train take the strain

One of the key green decisions a traveller can make is how they should travel. One of the best answers is to take public transport, such as buses or trains. The train company Eurostar is promoting the green credentials of railway travel through its 'Tread Lightly' initiative. The company runs trains through the Channel tunnel between Britain and France. On its website, the company claims that using its train service emits ten times less carbon dioxide than the equivalent flight.

The environmental pressure group, Friends of the Earth, is also advising Eurostar on ways to further reduce its impact on the environment. In turn, Eurostar is helping Friends of the Earth to build support for a really strong climate change law.

▼ Eurostar passengers leave a train. Eurostar has made a commitment to reduce its carbon dioxide emissions by 25 per cent per traveller journey by 2012.

Debate····· Can we rely on technology?

The environmental impact of many tourist journeys depends on the fuel-efficiency of the vehicles used. Technological improvements can go a long way to make individual journeys less polluting. For example, in recent years engineers have improved the fuel efficiency of aeroplanes. One of the most efficient is the Airbus A380. According to its manufacturer, when fully loaded it only uses the same amount of fuel as a family car to transport a passenger 100 km.

However, technology can only be part of any solution. Regardless of how efficient a plane is, it will still produce significant amounts of pollution and use significant amounts of fuel because of the number of passengers it carries and the distance it flies. Any overall gains that are made thanks to technological improvements can also be lost if more people decide to travel. This means that any solution to the tourism transport challenge cannot rely on technology alone.

The resource challenge

▼ Energy use by hotels and resorts, such as heating pools, contributes to global warming.

It's not just tourism transport that uses fuel and other resources; so do all of the other parts of the tourism industry, from the smallest guesthouse through to the largest mega-resort. Because the tourism industry is such a large, global industry, this resource use is a major environmental challenge.

The key resource issues

• Water: around the world the demand for water is growing rapidly, and water resources are becoming ever more stretched. Many tourist hotels, resorts and other facilities are big water users – they often have swimming pools and use large quantities of water to irrigate lush gardens and grounds. Water conservation is particularly important in places where water supplies are scarce or not well set up. In such places tourism developments can compete for water supplies with local people.

• Energy: tourist hotels and resorts are big energy users. When energy from fossil fuels (such as coal, gas and oil) is used to light, cool or heat a tourist hotel or other facility, it contributes to the release of pollution from power stations. This pollution includes carbon dioxide (the key global warming gas). It also leads to the depletion of energy resources. This means that, if tourism companies are serious about reducing their environmental impact, they must act to cut down the amount of energy they use across all their operations.

> 'An average 18-hole golf course soaks up at least 525,000 gallons of water a day – enough to supply the irrigation needs of 100 Malaysian farmers.'
>
> Tourism Concern

▼ Solar cookers, like this one, reduce the need for firewood and so help combat deforestation.

• Other resources: energy and water are not the only resources that tourism uses. Food, paper, cleaning materials, paints, concrete and wood are just some of the things that the tourism industry uses. All of these products require energy and other resources to produce them. Their production can also harm the environment and can produce pollution and waste. The products can also be polluting in their own right. It is possible to reduce the environmental impact of much of this resource use by choosing 'greener options', such as recycled paper, wood from sustainable sources and eco-friendly cleaning products.

Case study...... Meeting the mountain resource challenge

The use of resources by tourists often has a very direct impact on the surrounding environment. For example, resource use is an on-going challenge in the Himalayas. This is one of the world's most remote and beautiful regions and home to Mount Everest. It is visited by tens of thousands of trekkers each year.

One of the key problems that the area has faced is deforestation. This has been caused by people cutting down wood to provide fires to heat tourist lodges and camps, and to provide tourists with hot water. In 1986, the King Mahendra Trust for Nature Conservation launched the Annapurna Conservation Area Project to try and do something about this resource use problem.

Taking a 'bottom-up' approach that involves local people, the project has introduced a range of technology that helps reduce dependence on firewood. These include solar panels, kerosene stoves and micro-hydroelectricity generation equipment. The project has been funded by a trekking fee and with money from conservation groups, such as the WWF.

A smaller footprint

An increasing number of tourism businesses are making commitments to reduce their environmental footprint. Many are finding that saving resources (especially energy) can save them significant amounts of money on their bills. They can reduce the amount of energy, water and other resources they use in many ways.

Case study······

A company-wide approach

Resource saving needs commitment and good management. One tourism company that is showing what can be done is the Scandic hotel chain. The environmental impact of Scandic's operations can be seen on its website where the amount of energy, waste, water and carbon dioxide the company is using and producing is continuously updated.

www.scandichotels.com/About-Us/Responsible-living

The company takes a comprehensive approach to resource saving and waste reduction, from fitting water-efficient taps and showers in its hotels to purchasing electricity from renewable sources and furnishing its properties in line

Tourism businesses can:

• Use green technology, such as energy-efficient light bulbs (above), water-saving toilets and solar panels.

• Choose the most environmentally friendly options when they buy the products and services they use.

• Change the way they do things and the services they provide to reduce the amount of energy and resources they use, such as installing showers (right) instead of baths.

• Design their buildings to be energy and water efficient and construct them using materials that have a small environmental impact.

• Use food grown locally to reduce the energy used to transport it from 'field to fork'.

with the toughest environmental standards. The hotel has made savings of over 18 million euros thanks to its environmental work.

In 2007, Scandic announced a target of halving carbon dioxide emissions by 2011. The chain aims to have zero carbon dioxide emissions by 2025.

Water conservation at a resort level

According to the environmental pressure group WWF, the expansion of the tourism industry in the Mediterranean is helping to destroy valuable wetlands and is contributing to the depletion of the water supplies that local communities and farmers depend on. According to the group, tourists visiting the region consume between 300 and 850 litres of water per day. Tourism in the region is set to grow significantly and the WWF say that water consumption by tourists must be reduced.

▲ Over a million people flock to Calvia's beautiful beaches every year.

Case study······

Calvia, in the Balearic Islands, is a Mediterranean resort that has worked to control water consumption so that tourism in the region can be more sustainable. The municipality of Calvia (which receives over 1.2 million tourists a year) has improved the region's water distribution network, and promoted the reuse of water and the installation of water meters. Calvia also set up the Blue Brigades programme. This programme provides advice to tourists and residents on how to save water. According to WWF, between 1999 and 2001, Blue Brigade volunteers installed 5,000 water-saving systems – for free!

'No company can avoid taking responsibility for the environment and focusing on environmental issues. Scandic shall therefore lead the way and work continuously to promote both a reduction in our environmental impact and a better environment. Scandic shall actively contribute to a sustainable society.'

Scandic's environmental policy

Loved to death

Although many tourism developments are well managed and have much less environmental impact than many other types of industry, tourism can have a dramatic, direct impact on the natural environment.

Even individual tourists can damage the environment. For example, scuba divers can easily damage coral reefs and hill walkers can cause extensive erosion on footpaths. Animals can be particularly affected, even in protected areas: for example in some game parks in Africa, safari traffic has been shown to disturb wild animals.

In many destinations high tourist numbers threaten to damage the environment, and some regions are in danger of being 'loved to death'. Recently experts from National Geographic *Traveler* magazine reviewed the impact of tourism on all the major World Heritage Sites (places acknowledged as being the most important on the planet). They found some sites suffered from problems such as pollution, overcrowding and inappropriate development.

The impact of tourism depends on many things – the number of tourists, the activities and facilities they use and the nature of the areas they visit. The maximum number of people that may visit a tourist destination at the same time, without causing destruction of

▼ **Many beachfront areas, such as this one in Vietnam, have been purely designed for the tourist industry.**

the physical, economic, socio-cultural environment is called its 'carrying capacity'.

Controlling the impact of tourism

Controlling the impact of tourism often requires careful planning and can involve many organisations and individuals - from national and local governments to the individual tourism companies and visitors themselves.

Many tourism destinations are working to incorporate environmental protection into their overall development plans. This often involves zoning tourism areas, so that the scale and nature of development is strictly controlled, or in some nature reserves, completely banned. However, in many places the drive for economic development means that environmental concerns are not the top priority.

Case study......
Planning for tourism on the reef

The Great Barrier Reef in Australia is one of the natural wonders of the world, stretching over 344,000 km² along the east coast of Australia. It is home to an amazing diversity of coral, fish and other marine creatures. It is also under threat from a combination of factors which include global warming, pollution and over-fishing.

Almost seven million people visit the reef each year. To control the pressure of tourists on the reef there are restrictions on the size of groups and vessels that can visit certain parts of the reef. Zoning plans are also in place and define the activities that can occur in certain locations.

The WWF gave the zoning plans its 'Gift To The Earth' award in recognition of the role they play in conserving the environment. According to the group, over a third of the reef is now a marine sanctuary.

'A major disaster. The bay is jammed with endless low-end tourist boats servicing cheap group tours from China, all throwing garbage into the water, and creating a racket of sound pollution with their engines.'

An expert from National Geographic *Traveler* magazine on Ha Long Bay in Vietnam.

'Before visiting the Great Barrier Reef Marine Park, it is important you study the zoning map for the area you are visiting to be sure of the activities that you can do and where you can do them.'

Advice given to tourists by the Great Barrier Reef Marine Park Authority

The big clean-up

One of the key environmental challenges posed by tourism is pollution, waste and litter. Many tourist developments produce a lot of sewage which, if it is not properly treated, can damage the local environment and harm wildlife. Tourists and tourism are also responsible for large amounts of rubbish which must be collected and disposed of.

Mountains and coasts

Pollution and litter from tourism are a particularly big problem in coastal and mountain areas. For example, Mount Fuji in Japan is visited by more than 200,000 hikers a year. The litter that all these tourists create is a big challenge for the local government and many groups and projects have been set up to clean up the mountain. Every year many tonnes of rubbish are lifted off the mountain.

By the sea, the litter and pollution problem isn't confined to the dry land. Cruise ships produce a lot of waste, including sewage and dirty water. Partly as a result of campaigns by environmental groups, new international legislation has been introduced requiring cruise ships to be fitted with sewage treatment or containment equipment. This will not totally solve the problem, but it is a step in the right direction.

Blue Flag Award

The importance of a clean, pollution and litter-free environment to tourism is shown by the success of the Blue Flag Award. This is a prestigious international award scheme which tourists can use to help identify beaches with high-quality water.

Over the years the Blue Flag Award has acted as an incentive to many beach authorities to improve the quality of the coast, and that this hard work has led to a revival of coastlines and tourist beaches around the world. According to the organisation, In 2007, more than 3,300 tourism destinations in 37 countries achieved recognition under the award.

▼ **The number of beaches and marinas gaining Blue Flag status increases every year.**

Campaign......
Surfers Against Sewage

Surfers Against Sewage (SAS) has campaigned for many years to get the sewage that is pumped into Britain's seas properly treated.

Partly as a result of SAS' work, many coastal areas in the UK are cleaner because of a significant investment in full sewage treatment systems, such as ultra violet (UV) disinfection or microfiltration. According to the UK's Environment Agency, over 85 per cent of bathing waters now comply with the European Commission standards, compared with just 32 per cent in 1990.

Among SAS's most recent actions was the 'No Butts on the Beach' campaign. This was a joint initiative with the Marine Conservation Society to ask smokers to dispose of their cigarette ends responsibly and keep beaches 'butt-free'.

'Trillions of cigarette butts enter the water environment every year with potentially devastating effects on marine wildlife. Cigarette butts are not biodegradable as the filters are made of a type of plastic and so persist for many years. They have been found in the guts of whales, dolphins, sea birds, fish and turtles where they can leach toxic chemicals.'

Emma Snowden, MCS Litter Projects Co-ordinator

Reduce, reuse and recycle

Rubbish from hotels and tourist resorts can put a great strain on local waste disposal facilities and can cause a wide range of pollution and other problems. A lot of rubbish is simply buried in landfills. This wastes a lot of resources and is becoming increasingly difficult and expensive as landfill sites become harder to find.

Waste reuse, reduction and recycling offer important ways to decrease the amount of waste that must be thrown away. Many hotels and resorts are now working to put recycling systems in place (often with the help of local government authorities) and to reduce the amount of waste they produce.

▼ Members of Surfers Against Sewage display their campaign message with another kind of butt!

NO BUTTS
ON THE BEACH!!

Reducing the impact of tourists

▲ The Skyrail in Cairns travels silently above the rainforest.

There are a lot of specific steps being taken to reduce the physical impact of tourists on the environment. For example, in the Norfolk Broads in the UK, the speed of motor boats on some of the waterways is limited to stop noise pollution and problems caused by waves; in the Red Sea, environmental groups have put in special mooring buoys that help stop boat anchors damaging coral; while on popular tourist tracks in Australia's Snowy Mountains, duckboards have been put down to stop walkers' feet eroding particularly fragile parts of the landscape.

Tourist education

Many resorts also work to educate tourists about the environmental issues that are specific to the areas they are visiting. They also help them to act in a responsible way. For example, wildlife areas often have a code of conduct for visitors. Some resorts or tourism agencies also encourage tourists to support local conservation work which helps to repair some of the damage that tourism itself can cause.

All aboard the Skyrail

One of the more high-tech ways of reducing the impact tourists have on the environment can be found in the rainforest that grows in Cairns, Australia. Here, a 7.5 kilometre long gondola cableway, called the Skyrail, allows tourists to travel through the rainforest canopy without disturbing the animals and plants below them. At various points along the Skyrail, tourists can get out and walk through the forest on boardwalks. The Skyrail was opened in 1995 and is a 'world first'. It was built using helicopters to ferry in materials, so that minimal damage was done to the rainforest environment.

Tourism puts something back

The Lake District in the north west of England is one of the most popular tourist destinations in the UK. Tourism pressure causes a range of problems, including traffic congestion and hillside erosion. The Tourism and Conservation Partnership (TCP) works with tourism businesses to highlight the link between tourism and the environment.

> 'The model of "Visitor Payback" where visitors to the area are invited to donate just £1 each for local conservation projects, is an inspired idea.'
>
> Sue Savage, TCP's Partnership Manager.

The TCP encourages fundraising for landscape conservation, and the development of environmentally sustainable practices within the industry. Tourism businesses linked to the TCP often raise money by asking visitors to donate to local conservation projects (such as footpath restoration work) when they pay for their accommodation. With the help of the TCP, tourism businesses in the Lake District have raised over £1 million for conservation.

Tourism helps regeneration

At its best, well-planned tourism development can help regenerate an area. For example, in Blackstone Valley in the USA the local tourism council has taken an 'integrated, community-centred' approach to tourism that has helped to transform a polluted landscape and river into a beautiful place for people to visit.

This project was winner of the destination stewardship category in the 2008 Tourism For Tomorrow Awards. According to the World Travel and Tourism Council, which runs the Awards, the Blackstone Tourism Council has 'succeeded in uniting a community; awakening it to the need to preserve the natural, cultural and historical features of its physical surroundings'.

▼ Tourists enjoy walking on trails in Blackstone Valley, USA.

Greening the tourist

The way in which tourists behave when they travel and go on holiday is one of the key things that affects their impact on the environment. This means that tourism cannot be truly sustainable without the help of the tourists themselves.

▼ **Advertising can encourage tourists to help the environment.**

Tourists have a key role to play in dealing with almost all of the environmental challenges facing tourism – from doing their bit by travelling in the least polluting way to saving water.

Because of this, a lot is being done to 'green the tourist'. At its simplest, this involves putting up notices in hotel rooms asking people to turn off lights when not in use. This type of work also involves setting up certification schemes (like those discussed on pages 38–39) to help tourists choose holidays that are more environmentally friendly.

Buyer beware

Tourists buy souvenirs to remind them of their holidays. This can be a really positive thing as it can help support local communities and conservation projects. In some cases, however, buying souvenirs can be bad for the environment. Many tourists are offered products made from endangered or threatened animals or plants, or which are produced in ways that harm the environment. According to the conservation group WWF, coral, elephant ivory carvings, traditional Chinese medicine and snakeskin accessories are among the top illegal wildlife trade items bought as souvenirs.

Many groups supply information to help tourists avoid such products and make an informed decision about what to buy while abroad. One of these is TRAFFIC – the leading conservation agency that monitors the trade in wild plants and animals. Among its publications is a series of 'Buyer Beware' brochures filled with advice on what not to buy.

TRAFFIC
the wildlife trade monitoring network

Illegal trade is driving many of our wild species to extinction. Hunting, trading or possession of protected species of wildlife or its products is a criminal offence punishable by imprisonment up to 7 years and a hefty fine.

Shawls of Shame
Shahtoosh Shawls are tainted with the blood of *Chiru*, the Tibetan Antelope. Two to three *Chirus* are killed to make one shawl. Possession of this shawl without an ownership certificate is illegal in India and attracts heavy punishment.

DON'T BUY TROUBLE

▲ Tourists are offered products made from hardwood. Most conservation authorities recommend using caution when buying souvenirs.

'Many tourists could be unwittingly helping to push some of the world's most endangered species to the brink of extinction, all for the sake of an exotic souvenir. Our message is "if in doubt, don't buy".'

Heather Sohl, a wildlife trade officer at WWF-UK

Get a Green Passport

To encourage more sustainable tourism, the United Nations Environment Programme (UNEP) has set up a web-based 'Green Passport' for tourists who want to be greener. The website is full of useful information on how to plan a greener trip, how to travel in a way that has a minimal impact on the environment and what to do when you get to your destination to help local people and wildlife.

www.unep.fr/greenpassport

According to UNEP, by browsing the website, travellers will learn how to reduce their environmental footprint while they are on holiday.

Among the information available in the Green Passport are guidelines for how to snorkel without damaging underwater habitats, such as coral reefs; advice on how to make your holiday 'carbon neutral'; and the environmentally-friendly thing to do when you are caught short and there are no toilet facilities!

One key idea that the Green Passport promotes is the concept of 'slow travel'. The website encourages people to spend more time in each destination, to choose not to fly and to travel overland instead of taking to the skies. It even includes the adventures of 'slow travel bloggers' for inspiration.

Cultural impact

It is not just the natural environment that can suffer from tourist pressure – so can man-made treasures such as temples and other cultural artefacts. This impact is mainly physical, but in many places tourism also leads some people to view cultural treasures as simply a way to make money – rather than being spiritually or artistically important.

▼ A main street in Kandy, Sri Lanka. Kandy is a sacred city and is a cultural treasure in itself.

Cultural balance

Despite these challenges, tourism can bring tremendous economic gains to local communities and be a positive cultural force, leading to an increase in understanding between different people. It can also be a way in which local culture is given a boost, for example, by showing that local handicrafts or art are valued. However, local cultures are often fragile and the impact of tourism is something that is can be difficult to control.

Boosting local culture

Many tourists travel to see places that are culturally important, such as temples, cathedrals and historic cities. Many of these places have been placed on the World Heritage List. This highlights places that are considered to be of 'outstanding universal value' and includes man-made wonders such as the Statue of Liberty in the USA, the Taj Mahal in India and the sacred city of Kandy in Sri Lanka. The group that co-ordinates the World Heritage List is UNESCO (the United Nations Educational, Scientific and Cultural Organisation).

http://whc.unesco.org/en/list

Although inclusion on the list does not guarantee that a site is safe from harm, it does often serve as a catalyst for heritage preservation. Countries that have sites on the list are encouraged to draw up management plans

▲ The rice terraces of the Philippine Cordilleras are a World Heritage Site.

to ensure that their sites are preserved. UNESCO also makes about US$4 million available to help countries identify, preserve and promote World Heritage sites. The World Heritage List currently includes 878 sites in 145 countries.

A map to help heritage

One organisation that is working to preserve the culture and 'sense of place' of tourist destinations is the National Geographic Society in the USA. It is championing the idea of Geotourism – a type of tourism that emphasises the distinctiveness of a location, and which benefits visitors and residents alike.

To show the idea in action, the Society is producing a Geotourism MapGuide of the Greater Yellowstone National Park in the north-west United States. According to the group, such MapGuides are different from normal tourist maps because they highlight the natural, historic and cultural assets unique to an area. They therefore show what needs to be preserved for the future and encourage tourists to act responsibly. The Yellowstone map highlights the National Park's rich wildlife alongside its cultural history, which is rooted in Native American tribal heritage and the exploits of explorers, ranchers, farmers and miners.

Tourism and wildlife conservation

Tourism can have a big negative impact on the natural environment and on wildlife. However, it can also provide money for conservation – offering a powerful economic justification for wildlife protection. This makes tourism a realistic alternative to potentially more destructive forms of industry, such as mining and forestry. In fact, in some cases it is one of the main reasons that wilderness areas are set aside as nature reserves or given similar protection.

Tourism supporting conservation

Tourism can help pay directly for conservation. For example, in Rwanda's Parc des Volcans, tourists pay hundreds of dollars to see mountain gorillas. This income is vital to help protect the gorillas against poaching and to manage their habitat.

However, as tourist numbers grow it is getting more difficult to control the negative impact of tourism on wildlife. A recent report on tourism and biodiversity from UNEP and Conservation International shows that many countries in the southern hemisphere, which are home to key 'biodiversity hotspots', are experiencing very rapid tourism growth: 23 of them experienced tourism growth of over 100 per cent in the last 10 years.

Whale watching

According to Greenpeace, whale watching occurs in more than 87 different countries and provides a sustainable source of income for many people. Whale watching lets people learn about these amazing animals. It is also a powerful tool for their conservation. This is vital as many whales are threatened by marine pollution, over-fishing and illegal whaling.

▼ **Tourists watching humpback whales. Thanks to tourism, wildlife often has more economic value alive and in its natural habitat than it would do if it was killed and processed.**

Debate······
Are hunting holidays worth it?

Some people enjoy hunting and go on holiday to shoot 'big game'. In some African countries, such as South Africa and Botswana, tourists pay thousands of dollars to get permission to shoot elephants and other wildlife.

Those in favour of licensed hunting argue that it takes place in regions where animal populations are healthy, and that it brings in much needed money that can be used for conservation. Those against hunting think that it is cruel and that it has a negative impact on natural animal populations. They believe that everything should be done to protect wild animals so that they can live undisturbed by humans.

Why should big game hunts go on even if the money is used for conservation? How, if at all, is this a sustainable solution?

▲ A tourist on a hunting holiday in Africa shows off his kill.

▼ Examples of hotspot countries with tourism growth of more than 100 per cent.

Hotspot/Country	International Arrivals (in thousands)			Growth 1990–2000 (in thousands)	Percentage Growth 1990–2000
	1990	1995	2000		
Indo-Burma					
Laos	14	60	300	286	2,043
Myanmar	21	117	208	87	890
Vietnam	250	1,351	2,140	1,890	756
Macao	2,513	4,202	6,682	4,169	166
Succulent Karoo/Cape Floristic Region					
South Africa	1,029	4,684	6,001	4,972	483
Caribbean					
Cuba	327	742	1,700	1,373	420
Turks and Caicos Islands	49	79	156	107	218
Dominican Republic	1,305	1,776	2,977	1,672	128
Brazilian Cerrado/Atlantic Forest					
Brazil	1,091	1,991	5,313	4,222	387
Mesoamerica					
Nicaragua	106	281	486	380	358
El Salvador	194	235	795	601	310
Costa Rica	435	785	1,106	671	154
Panama	214	345	479	265	124
Guinean Forests					
Nigeria	190	656	813	623	328
Tropical Andes					
Peru	317	541	1,027	710	224
Madagascar and Indian Ocean Islands					
Madagascar	53	75	160	107	202
Eastern Arc Mountains and Coastal Forests					
Tanzania, United Republic of	153	285	459	306	200
Mountains of Southwest China					
China	10,484	20,034	31,229	20,745	198
Sundaland/Wallacea					
Indonesia	2,178	4,324	5,064	2,886	133
Mediterranean Basin					
Israel	1,063	2,215	2,400	1,337	126
Southwest Australia					
Australia	2,215	3,726	4,946	2,731	123
Micronesia/Polynesia					
Cook Islands	34	48	73	39	115

Tourism, wildlife and people

I t is increasingly being understood that conservation works best with the support and involvement of local people. Unfortunately in the past, some conservation projects have excluded local people leading to them being removed from their land to create wildlife areas, and forcing them to poach wildlife. Because of this, more and more wildlife conservation projects that involve tourism are now being based on a partnership model.

▲ Local people in the Masai Mara can earn money by acting as tourist guides. They have an unrivaled knowledge of the local area.

Money for honey

One group that is working to make a difference to the lives of local people who live near a wildlife conservation area is Friends of Conservation (FOC). Founded in 1982, FOC was originally established to help prevent wildlife and habitat destruction in the Masai Mara – one of Africa's most famous wildlife areas. The group has set up educational and support programmes for local people, including an arts and crafts project. This works with local Masai women to help them make traditional leather and beadwork which they can sell to tourists. FOC also works with a number of women's groups to develop bee-keeping skills. The honey that is produced is sold to lodges on the Masai Mara reserve and in nearby towns. This means that local people can make money from tourism.

Local ownership equals local conservation

The Posadas Amazonas lodge sits in the middle of the Amazon rainforest in Peru. Tourists visit the lodge to enjoy being amongst the amazing wildlife that lives in the surrounding forest. This includes macaws, giant river otters and eagles.

The lodge is part owned by the local Ese'eja Indian community, who are involved in its management and receive some 60 per cent of the profits. Local people also make up most of the staff of the lodge. Because the success of the lodge depends upon the conservation of the surrounding forest, the project gives local people an added incentive to support and get involved with the conservation of the wildlife they live amongst.

▲ Watching a sea turtle on the beach. Local people can be employed as guides and play an active role in turtle conservation.

Turtle conservation, tourism and communities

Sea turtles in Sri Lanka are endangered because of factors such as habitat destruction, illegal egg collection and fishing. The country's Turtle Conservation Project (TCP) aims to help the turtles survive in the face of these ever increasing pressures.

The TCP works closely with local people to educate them on the plight of the turtles. It also helps provide them with work linked to turtle conservation, so they have a reason to save the turtles.

To do this, the TCP runs a number of nature tourism programmes and trains and employs local people as guides. These programmes consist of tourist activities, such as bird watching, coral study and night time 'turtle watches', in which tourists can see the turtles nesting. The TCP also employs people who used to poach turtle eggs as nest protectors on beaches. This project is a great example of how tourism can provide a way for local people to be involved in conservation.

'We believe that if we help to support the alleviation of poverty through diversifying environmentally sustainable income generating activities, communities themselves will not only be able to reduce destructive practices carried out on the environment but also be encouraged to see it as a financial asset.'

Friends of Conservation

Eco-tourists – a new type of traveller?

One of the fastest growing areas of tourism involves holidays that are designed to let people visit and experience wildlife and wild environments in a way that does as little harm as possible. One of the names given to this type of approach is 'eco-tourism' and it is hoped by many that this represents an environmentally-friendly future for tourism. Unfortunately, some tourism operators are using the 'eco-tourism' label as a marketing strategy to sell holidays that still damage the environment and exploit people.

'The definition of eco-tourism makes a high claim for its positive impact on society and the environment. It is important that these principles are properly implemented and continue to show the way for others.'

From the Oslo Statement on Eco-tourism

▼ Watching gorillas on an eco-tourist holiday.

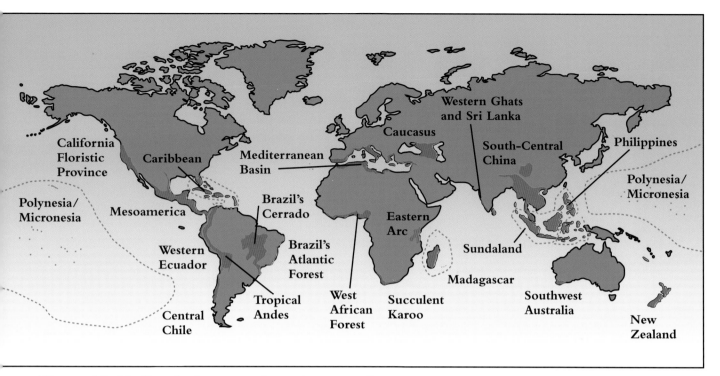

▲ The world's biodiversity hotspots, shown here, are all potential destinations for eco-tourists.

What is eco-tourism?

The International Eco-Tourism Society (TIES) defines eco-tourism as 'responsible travel to natural areas that conserves the environment and improves the well-being of local people.' TIES says that eco-tourism is about uniting conservation, communities and sustainable travel, and that any eco-tourism activity should:

- minimise impact
- build environmental and cultural awareness and respect
- provide positive experiences for both visitors and hosts
- provide direct financial benefits for conservation
- provide financial benefits and empowerment for local people
- raise sensitivity to host countries' political, environmental and social climate.

This means that a rainforest trekking holiday is not necessarily eco-tourism, unless it raises awareness about rainforest conservation and funds for such work.

In 2007, the inaugural Global Eco-tourism Conference was held in Norway. One of the key outcomes of this meeting was the Oslo Statement on Eco-tourism, which set out the steps that should be taken to maximise the positive benefits of the approach.

The eco-tourism idea draws together all of the positive benefits that tourism can have for conservation. As we've seen, tourism to biodiversity hot spots is set to grow. These hotspots are also coming under ever increasing pressure from a wide range of other environmental problems. This means that eco-tourism,

done correctly, has the potential to be a very powerful tool for conservation in years to come.

Holidays for the planet

Many tourists do more than just visit wild areas to see the sights. A growing number of intrepid travellers actually get involved in conservation work. For example, Coral Cay Conservation is a group that sets up expeditions for groups of amateur divers to do coral reef research and conservation work in places such as the Philippines.

Another group that does this kind of work is the Earthwatch Institute. This organisation provides an opportunity for people to get directly involved in conservation by working alongside leading scientists in some of the wildest places on Earth.

Tourism and sustainable development

Tourism supports over 200 million jobs worldwide, and has a massive impact on people's livelihoods. For this reason, many groups are working to ensure that tourism is 'pro-poor', and promotes the economic well-being of local people. It is only by helping people economically that a sustainable tourism project can provide a true alternative to other, more environmentally damaging, ways of making a living. If people truly benefit from sustainable tourism, they will also be much more supportive of its aims and objectives.

The social challenge

Unfortunately, the economic benefits of tourism are not equally shared. According to the UN, in many less developed countries much of the profits of tourism do not benefit the host country. For example, it is thought that in some African countries up to 85 per cent of profits 'leak' out to developed nations through companies, such as airlines, hotel chains and other supply companies. This means that local people, who are often employed in low-wage jobs such as cleaning rooms or pools (below left), do not get as much benefit from tourism as they might.

Tourism can also have other negative economic effects on local people. For example, tourism can cause a rise in property prices, forcing local people to move away because they cannot afford to buy a home.

▼ **This graph shows the number of jobs (in 000's) in the tourism industry worldwide – from 1988 to forecast numbers in 2013.**

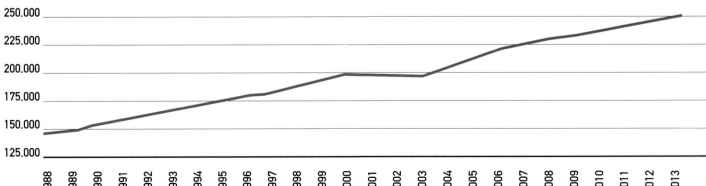

Campaign.....
Helping the poor take a ST-EP forward

The World Tourism Organisation (UNWTO – a United Nations organisation) is working to highlight the important role that sustainable tourism can play in raising people's standard of living. To kick start this work, it launched the ST-EP (Sustainable Tourism – Eliminating Poverty) initiative at the World Summit for Sustainable Development in Johannesburg in 2002.

The ST-EP initiative focuses on how tourism can reduce poverty levels by delivering development and jobs to people living on less than a dollar or two a day. As part of this, the UNWTO has set up a number of ST-EP projects to provide practical help for the poor.

According to the UNWTO, these projects include schemes that focus on training guides and local hotel employees, and which help local people get involved in the development of tourism around natural and cultural heritage sites. Projects also help forge links to local producers.

For example, in the Lao People's Democratic Republic, ST-EP projects are supporting the development of village-based tourism and helping local women market and sell the high quality textiles they weave to tourists.

'Poverty alleviation has become an essential condition for peace, environmental conservation and sustainable development, besides being an ethical obligation in an affluent world, where the divide between poor and rich nations seems to have increased in recent years.'

UNWTO

▲ Initiatives, such as ST-EP, have helped local people to benefit directly from tourism. Simply assisting people in getting their hand-made products to market can dramatically reduce poverty levels.

Fair trade tourism

To be pro-poor, tourism must not only provide people with a fair wage and a good livelihood, it must also provide fair working conditions. Some people involved in tourism are made to work in poor conditions that are unsafe or which can damage their health. Women and children in less developed countries are particularly at risk from this kind of exploitation.

▼ The 3 Sisters help to train local women as guides so that they can earn an income.

Case study·····
Helping women

A group called 3 Sisters Adventure Trekking is working to try and do something about the economic plight of women in Nepal. The group uses tourism to provide women with an income and to bring revenue to the poorest areas of the country.

It does this by helping women to train to become adventure professionals and acquire the skills to earn money, interact with the world, and discover their own strength. According to the group – which prides itself on being the only 100 per cent woman-owned and

operated trekking agency in Nepal – women in the country are typically excluded from tourism, which is one of Nepal's top industries. In all its work, 3 Sisters aims to promote tourism that does not damage people's cultural identities or the environment.

Campaign.....
Trekking wrongs: porter's rights

One of the key organisations campaigning for workers' rights in the tourism industry is Tourism Concern. Among the issues it has highlighted are the poor working conditions, illnesses and injury suffered by porters who carry tourists' equipment in mountain areas, such as the Inca Trail in Peru and Mount Kilimanjaro, Tanzania.

To try and help the porters, Tourism Concern worked to publicise their plight through its 'Trekking Wrongs: Porter's Rights' campaign. This targetted tourists, the trekking industry and tour operators within the UK. The group's campaign has got results. According to the group over half of UK trekking tour operators have now adopted its code of conduct for improved working conditions for mountain porters. Tourism Concern advises tourists who are thinking of going on a trekking holiday to use these companies – supporting ethical tourism and the porters themselves.

'Until Tourism Concern told our stories, no-one took us seriously. We were thought of as pack animals.'

A porter, Nepal

▶ Porters, like this one, help to carry tourist equipment and supplies. For many years they have been unfairly treated and poorly paid.

Promoting fair trade

Many people buy 'fair trade' products to support companies that provide a fair deal to their workers. Now this idea is being used to support workers' rights in tourism. A leader in this field is Fair Trade in Tourism South Africa (FTTSA). The group lets qualifying businesses use a special label to show that they are committed to fair trade ideals. These include fair wages and working conditions, fair distribution of benefits and respect for human rights, culture and the environment.

The Klippe Rivier Country House is a company that has been given the FTTSA label. The majority of staff at this guest house in South Africa's Western Cape were from disadvantaged, rural backgrounds, who have since received training and gained secure employment. Klippe Rivier also supports small businesses and buys local produce. Guests are encouraged to visit local art and craft businesses. According to the FTTSA, by electing to stay at or use the services of an FTTSA-certified establishment, tourists are assured that their travel benefits local communities and that the business is operated ethically and in a socially and environmentally responsible manner.

Awarding sustainable tourism

▲ This quad bike tour in New Zealand has a Green Globe certificate.

To give sustainable tourism a helping hand, a number of schemes have been set up to help tourism operators reduce their environmental impact, and to help tourists choose the most environmentally-friendly holidays.

Green schemes

Some of these schemes involve laying down green guidelines for tourism operations and there are many organisations that give advice to companies and destinations on how to 'go green'.

Other schemes vet tourism operations on a range of environmental criteria, such as energy, water and resource use, waste management and ecological impact. They then give awards or certification to companies or destinations that achieve a certain standard.

One of the largest green tourism certification systems is Green Globe, which was set up by the World Travel and Tourism Council in 1994. Organisations that take part in the Green Globe programme are given an 'action framework' they can use to measure, monitor, manage and improve their environmental and social performance. Depending on how far they get within the scheme, participants are given different levels of certification. This allows them to show their commitment to sustainable tourism and the environment.

Schemes such as Green Globe are important because they give companies an added incentive to become more sustainable. This is because they can use their involvement in the scheme as part of their marketing – using their green credentials to attract new customers.

The whole field of environmental certification faces some tough challenges. Many critics say that there are currently too many different schemes in operation and that tourists can be confused. There is also controversy about what level of environmental protection should merit recognition by an award and what range of actions should be judged.

Eco-tourism Australia

Eco-tourism is one of the fastest growing tourism sectors and, perhaps, one of the most difficult to evaluate (see pages 32–33). Eco-tourism Australia is a scheme that aims to do just that. It provides certification to eco-tourism and wildlife-tourism companies, tours and attractions that have passed a strict assessment process. The organisation also runs an eco-guide certification programme which, it says, endorses guides

'who will deliver an authentic, environmentally responsible, and professional eco-tourism experience'.

The scheme boasts over 700 eco-certified operators and

members – the organisation covers every state in Australia. In 2008, Eco-tourism Australia was awarded the prestigious World Travel and Tourism Council 'Tourism for Tomorrow' Award for Conservation.

▲ Eco-tourists can take part in a range of activities, such as this tour of volcanic White Island, New Zealand.

'The Eco Certification Program is a world first. It has been developed by industry for industry, addressing the need to identify genuine eco-tourism and nature tourism operators in Australia.'

Eco-tourism Australia

A sustainable future for tourism?

Tourism is at a pivotal moment in its development. On the one hand, many people are worried about the impact it has on wildlife, the environment, and on local cultures and people. On the other hand, it is becoming clear that if it is done in a sustainable way, tourism can provide an environmentally-friendly way for many people to improve their lives and for countries to develop.

▲ **A tourist steps out across a swing bridge on a rainforest walk.**

Shaping the future

However, delivering on the promise of sustainable tourism remains a real challenge. It requires an approach that brings together many different elements, including local and national governments, tourism operators, conservation groups and tourists themselves. It needs significant investment in terms of technology and infrastructure, time and expertise; it also requires people and companies to agree that environmental concerns should be given high priority – often over and above immediate economic concerns. None of these challenges are easy. However, as environmental pressures around the world continue to grow, so sustainable tourism will become ever more important and demand for it will grow – from governments, campaign groups and the general public. Pioneering companies, groups and individuals have shown the way. How the rest of the industry follows will shape the future, not only of tourism but also of the planet.

'Far sighted action by the US$880 billion international tourism industry will send important signals to governments, industries and the public that mitigation and adaptation to the climate change challenge make economic and environmental sense. It is the kind of leadership that can encourage others to look not only to their exposure and to the risks posed by climate change, but also to the abundant opportunities and benefits of cost effective action.'

Achim Steiner, UN Under-Secretary General and UNEP Executive Director.

Debate·····
The global warming challenge – what else needs to be done?

Global warming is probably the key challenge facing tourism in the immediate future. This was highlighted by the fact that the theme of World Tourism Day 2008 was 'Tourism Responding to the Challenge of Climate Change'. The challenge facing tourism is set out in the Davos Declaration put together by the UN World Tourism Organisation and other leading tourism and environmental bodies. It says that the tourism industry must rapidly respond to climate change, if it is to grow in a sustainable manner. According to the declaration, this will require the industry to:

● mitigate its greenhouse gas emissions, derived especially from transport and accommodation;
● adapt tourism businesses and destinations to changing climate conditions;
● apply existing and new technology to improve energy efficiency;
● secure financial resources to help poor regions and countries.

▼ World Tourism Day – Tourism Responding to the Challenge of Climate Change – took place in Peru and featured different cultural events, including traditional dance.

Case study·····
A future green resort

A glimpse of what the future for sustainable tourism might hold is on the drawing boards of a tourism developer in Portugal. The Mata de Sesimbra eco-tourism project will transform an area of degraded logging plantations and quarries into a 48 km² nature reserve and sustainable tourism resort.

According to Bioregional (one of a number of environmental groups working with the project) the resort will be powered completely by renewable energy, will aim to reduce the amount of waste going to landfill to 5 per cent of the national average, and will dramatically cut its use of water by collecting rain and recycling waste water. Half of the resort's building materials will have been recycled and half of all the food served will be grown locally. A sustainable public transport network is also planned – it will include hybrid eco-shuttles, free bicycles and car clubs.

Tourism
Responding to the Challenge of
Climate Change
w w w . u n w t o . o r g

Glossary

biodiversity: the variety of plants, animals and other forms of life that exist in a certain place.

carbon dioxide: a gas that naturally occurs in the Earth's atmosphere. Carbon dioxide is released when fossil fuels, such as coal, oil and gas are burned.

carbon offsetting: buying products or services which help reduce the emission of carbon dioxide to help combat global warming.

climate change: long-term, significant change in the world's climate. Many scientists now believe that man-made greenhouse gases, such as carbon dioxide, are responsible for climate change.

conservation: the protection of the health and well-being of the natural world, including habitats and the wildlife that lives in them.

coral reefs: large underwater structures made by coral animals and their skeletons. Coral reefs are predominantly found in tropical waters and are home to a vast number of fish and other marine life.

duckboard: a walkway made of boards that is used to help people cross muddy ground.

eco-tourism: responsible travel to natural areas that conserves the environment and improves the well-being of local people.

environmental footprint: a measure of the environmental impact of a person or activity in terms of the amount of natural resources they use and the amount of pollution they produce.

ethical: an action that is fair or just. Ethical tourism is tourism that does not exploit people and which gives people a fair return for any work they do.

fair trade: a social and economic approach that aims to help people, particularly in developing countries, by, primarily, providing them with a fair price for the goods they make.

geotourism: a type of tourism that emphasizes the distinctiveness of a location, and which benefits visitors and residents alike.

global warming: an increase in the average measured temperature of the Earth. Many scientists now believe that man-made greenhouse gases, such as carbon dioxide, are responsible for global warming.

independent traveller: a tourist who arranges his or her own itinerary and transport arrangements and usually travels alone or in a small group.

poaching: the illegal hunting, fishing or collecting of wild plants or animals.

pollution: contaminants that cause harm, damage or discomfit to the environment or living things.

recycling: the processing of old or used materials into new raw materials or products. Recycling helps cut down waste, preserves natural resources and reduces pollution.

sewage: liquid waste produced by humans, sewage is made up of the material that is flushed down the toilet and emptied into drains.

sustainable: an activity is environmentally sustainable if it can continue to take place without causing lasting damage to the environment.

zoning plans: a plan which divides a location up into different zones in which only certain activities can take place.

Websites

Blue Flag
www.blueflag.org
The scheme that vets the quality of beaches around the world and awards those that meet strict environmental standards.

Great Barrier Reef Marine Park Authority
www.gbrmpa.gov.au
The organisation in charge of looking after Australia's Great Barrier Reef. Find out how they do it.

Green Globe
www.greenglobe21.com
The scheme that gives awards to tourism companies that provide products and services that meet certain environmental criteria.

Scandic Hotel
www.scandic-campaign.com/
livereport/?lang=en
The environmental website of the Scandic Hotel group. It explains what the organisation does to reduce its environmental impact and has a 'live' display of the company's green performance.

Surfers Against Sewage (SAS)
www.sas.org.uk
The website of one of the coolest environmental groups around which campaigns for clean seas and beaches.

The International Eco-Tourism Society (TIES)
www.ecotourism.org
The website of the world's oldest and largest eco-tourism organisation. TIES is committed to promoting the principles of eco-tourism and responsible travel.

Tourism Concern
www.tourismconcern.org.uk
A leading campaign groups that highlights many of the environmental and social problems that tourism has caused and works to solve them.

Tourism For Tomorrow Awards
www.tourismfortomorrow.com
An international award scheme that highlights the most environmentally friendly tourism businesses from around the world – find out who the latest winners are.

Green Passport
www.unep.fr/greenpassport
A website full of information and tips on how to be a green tourist.

World Heritage List
whc.unesco.org/en/list
The list of World Heritage Sites – the most important places in the world.

World Tourism Organisation (UNWTO)
www.world-tourism.org
The website of the leading international organisation in the field of tourism. It serves as a global forum for tourism policy issues and a practical source of tourism know-how.

World Wildlife Fund (WWF)
www.wwf.org
The official site of one of the world's leading conservation organisations.

Please note: every effort has been made by the Publishers to ensure that these websites contain no inappropriate or offensive material. However, because of the nature of the Internet, it is impossible to guarantee that the contents of these sites will not be altered. We strongly advise that Internet access is supervised by a responsible adult.

Index